YORK NOTES

# Seamus Heaney
# Selected Poems

Notes by Shay Daly

 Longman      York Press

YORK PRESS
322 Old Brompton Road, London SW5 9JH

Pearson Education Limited
Edinburgh Gate, Harlow,
Essex CM20 2JE, United Kingdom
Associated companies, branches and representatives throughout the world

First published 1998
Eighth impression 2006

ISBN-10: 0-582-36821-9
ISBN-13: 978-0-582-36821-7

Designed by Vicki Pacey, Trojan Horse, London
Illustrated by Chris Brown
Phototypeset by Gem Graphics, Trenance, Mawgan Porth, Cornwall
Colour reproduction and film output by Spectrum Colour
Produced by Pearson Education Asia Limited, Hong Kong

# ONTENTS

# PREFACE

York Notes are designed to give you a broader perspective on works of literature studied at GCSE and equivalent levels. We have carried out extensive research into the needs of the modern literature student prior to publishing this new edition. Our research showed that no existing series fully met students' requirements. Rather than present a single authoritative approach, we have provided alternative viewpoints, empowering students to reach their own interpretations of the text. York Notes provide a close examination of the work and include biographical and historical background, summaries, glossaries, analyses of characters, themes, structure and language, cultural connections and literary terms.

If you look at the Contents page you will see the structure for the series. However, there's no need to read from the beginning to the end as you would with a novel, play, poem or short story. Use the Notes in the way that suits you. Our aim is to help you with your understanding of the work, not to dictate how you should learn.

York Notes are written by English teachers and examiners, with an expert knowledge of the subject. They show you how to succeed in coursework and examination assignments, guiding you through the text and offering practical advice. Questions and comments will extend, test and reinforce your knowledge. Attractive colour design and illustrations improve clarity and understanding, making these Notes easy to use and handy for quick reference.

York Notes are ideal for:
- Essay writing
- Exam preparation
- Class discussion

The author of these Notes is Shay Daly. After leaving school to become a professional actor, Shay studied English and Drama at De La Salle College and Manchester University. He has taught in Manchester for over twenty years, first as Head of Drama and now as Head of English at Barlow High School in Didsbury. He is Senior Examiner and Moderator for an Examination Board.

The text used in these Notes is *Seamus Heaney, New Selected Peoms 1966–1987*, Faber and Faber, 1990.

*Health Warning:* **This study guide will enhance your understanding, but should not replace the reading of the original text and/or study in class.**

# PART ONE

# INTRODUCTION

## HOW TO STUDY A POEM

You have bought this book because you wanted to study poetry on your own. This may supplement work done in class.

- Look at the poem. How are the lines organised? Are they in groups? Are any lines repeated? Are any of the lines shorter or longer than the others? Try to think of reasons why the poet set out the lines in this way.

- Do lots of the lines end with a comma or a full stop – or does the sense carry over on to another line? What is the effect of stopping at the end of each line?

- Read the poem out aloud (or aloud in your head). Does the poem rhyme? If so, what words rhyme? Is this important ? Do some lines almost rhyme? Do some lines have rhyming words inside the line? If there is no rhyme, think about why the poet stops each line where he/she does.

- Read the poem aloud again. Think about the rhythm. Listen for the stressed words. Does the pattern of stressed and unstressed syllables create any kind of mood? Does it match the mood or subject-matter of the poem? Have some words been chosen for their sound?

- What is the poem about? Do not make up your mind too soon. Your first thoughts need to be reassessed when you reach the end. Remember that the subject-matter and the theme or idea of the poem may not be the same.

- Do any words make you stop and think? Are there interesting or unusual combinations of words? (Check the meaning of any words which puzzle you – they may have a meaning you are not familiar with.)

Seamus Heaney was born in the townland of Tamnairn, at Mossbawn, County Derry, Northern Ireland, on 13 April 1939. He was the eldest of nine children, one of whom died in a road accident and is remembered in the poem 'Mid-Term Break'. His father was a farmer and therefore he lived all his young life on a farm. Much of the raw material for his poetry stems from the farm and the countryside around the farm. Seamus Heaney himself, even though he admired the skill and dedication of his father and grandfather (see 'Follower' and 'Digging') did not wish to follow his ancestors in the family tradition.

*The poet's early life and first poems*

He attended primary school in Anahorish (see the poem of the same name) and it was here that he was introduced to the literary greats. From this school he won a scholarship to St Columb's College in Londonderry. He was a boarder at St Columb's from 1951 to 1957. He attended Queen's University, Belfast, and was awarded a first class honours degree in English Language and Literature. His first published work appeared in the university magazine under the pseudonym 'Insertus'. He was now heavily under the influence of Philip Hobsbaum, a man who gathered a group of like-minded young people to read poetry and talk about literature. It was here that Seamus Heaney met his future wife, Marie Devlin.

*First published work.*

He began his teaching career at St Thomas's Secondary School, Belfast, and then went on to St Joseph's Technical College. It was during this period that he began to develop as a poet. A number of his poems were published in the *New Statesman* and in other London magazines. He married Marie in 1965 and they have two sons, Michael and Christopher and a daughter, Catherine Ann.

*Death of a Naturalist*, Seamus Heaney's first collection of poetry, was published in 1966, while he was a

*Death of a*
*Naturalist*
*published.*

lecturer at Queen's University. It was immediately accepted as a remarkable work of literature. Seamus Heaney was just twenty-seven years old. The collection is concerned with the loss of childhood innocence and the movement into adulthood and all that such a 'journey' implies. The poetry also shows the reader glimpses of his reasons for being a writer, his admiration for his ancestors and the young Seamus Heaney's distorted view of nature.

*Seamus Heaney is*
*becoming more*
*confident.*

Seamus Heaney's second collection, *Door into the Dark*, was published in 1969. The poetry was just that, a step into the unknown, the step of a poet who was sufficiently confident to take risks and know that he would be successful. He writes about Irish history, Irish myths and the Irish people and attempts to create a literary, mystical vision.

While at Berkeley University, California, he read the poets Gary Snyder and Robert Bly. Their use of **free verse** (see Literary Terms) had some influence on his writing in his next collection, *Wintering Out*, which was published in 1972.

**Seamus**
**Heaney**
**becomes a**
**full-time**
**writer.**

It was at about this time that he decided to become a full-time writer. After resigning his teaching post at Queen's University he and his family went to live at Ashford, County Wicklow, in Ireland. It was here that he began the translation of 'The Lament of Mad Sweeney', which he entitled 'Sweeney Astray'. This version was published much later, in 1983.

The poems in *North*, which were published in 1975, confront the situation in the North of Ireland directly and nowhere is this seen more obviously than in the poem 'Whatever You Say, Say Nothing'. In this collection the reader sees a personal response to the problems of the North.

In 1976 he accepted a post as Head of English 'at Carysfort Teachers' Training College and then in 1982 he became Poet in Residence at Harvard University. Seamus Heaney was appointed as Professor of Poetry at Oxford University and remained in that post until 1994.

He has also written four further collections of poetry: *Station Island* (1984), *The Haw Lantern* (1987), *Seeing Things* (1991) and his latest, *The Spirit Level*, which was completed and published in 1996.

*Nobel Prize for Literature*    The previous year Seamus Heaney was awarded the Nobel Prize for Literature in recognition of his literary genius and 'for works of lyrical beauty and ethical depth which exalt everyday miracles and the living past'.

## Context & setting

The study of Seamus Heaney's poetry demands that we comprehend the struggles against oppression that have occurred throughout Irish history and in particular from the twelfth century onwards.

*Normans invade Ireland*    The Normans occupied parts of Ireland during the twelfth century and since that time England (and now the United Kingdom) has been involved to a greater or lesser degree in the government of Ireland.

During the sixteenth century the great Earls of Ulster, Hugh O'Neil, Earl of Tyrone and Hugh O'Donnell, Earl of Tyrconnel, led an insurrection against Queen Elizabeth I and her country. Unfortunately for them the aid they expected from their Spanish allies did not arrive in time and the Earls had to surrender. This was followed by the 'Flight of Earls' to the continent of Europe.

Ulster was regarded as a dangerous place by the English crown and when James I came to the throne he claimed the huge tracts of land owned by the Earls and colonised these areas with English subjects. Historically this was the time when the English established their claims to six counties in the North of Ireland although they were not exactly the same counties that are part of the United Kingdom today.

*Oliver Cromwell*

The seventeenth century was a fateful one in the history of Ireland. England felt that its authority in Ireland was being undermined. Catholics were in a strong position because of the rise of the Catholic Spanish Empire and also the power of the Vatican. Oliver Cromwell was prepared to destroy the strength of the Catholics and his name has become a byword for savagery whenever this period in Irish history is mentioned. He was responsible for the deaths of three thousand Catholics when he arrived in Drogheda and for many more when he attacked Wexford. Later, he awarded land in Ireland to those who were loyal to his cause.

*Battle of the Boyne*

The tide was reversed for a short time in favour of the Catholics when James II came to the throne. Earl Tyrconnell, a Catholic, was appointed Lord Lieutenant and he immediately set about removing Protestants from the army. He then weakened the army by sending troops to support James II in England. It was now that the seeds of the present troubles in Northern Ireland were sown. The discontented Protestants in the North invited William of Orange to help their cause. When he became King of England the Protestants had a powerful figurehead as their leader. William of Orange fought and defeated James II in 1690 at the Battle of the Boyne. This victory gave the Protestants the power they required to rule the country. Catholics were now denied the right to vote or even to own their own land.

Eventually the deep discontent of the Catholics, and indeed some Protestants and Presbyterians, led to the founding of the United Irishmen. They fought a battle against their Protestant rulers in Armagh but were defeated and it was after this battle that the Orange Society was created. The aim of this society was to ensure that Protestants always held the upper hand over the Catholics.

*Battle of Vinegar Hill*

A number of other battles were fought but the rebellion was poorly organised. The battle of Vinegar Hill saw the rebels' greatest and bloodiest defeat. Twenty thousand men died in May 1798. The rule of law had almost completely broken down and this encouraged the authorities to set up the Act of Union to unite the English and Irish governments. When the bill was passed in 1800 many of the big landlords who opposed the union moved to England and allowed their managers to run the estates.

*The famine*

During the 1840s Ireland suffered one of the greatest disasters in its history. The majority of the population depended on the potato for food and when the crop failed for three years famine spread throughout the land. In the latter half of the 1840s over a million people died and many more emigrated to America. The 'Coffin Ships', as they were called, claimed even more lives. The population of Ireland was halved in the space of a few years.

William Gladstone (1809–98) was convinced that Home Rule was essential if the problems in Ireland were to be solved. Throughout the nineteenth century and the early twentieth century Protestants opposed the idea of Home Rule because they saw it as the end of Protestant ascendancy. Two rebel groups were formed. The Ulster Volunteers were a force dedicated to the Protestant cause and the nationalists created their own group called the Irish Volunteers. This latter group declared itself to be dedicated to protection but the Irish Republican Brotherhood (IRB) seized the General Post Office in Dublin in Easter 1916 and proclaimed the Irish Republic. The IRB soon surrendered and twelve of its leaders were executed. These executions aroused great sympathy and the mass of the Catholic population now supported the rebels.

*Partition*

Civil war broke out in 1920 and the English government was powerless to create any stability. In the same year partition was set up. The North and South were to have their own parliaments. This was regarded as a temporary measure at the time but eventually the borders were clearly defined. The country is now divided in two, the six counties of Northern Ireland and the twenty-six counties of Southern Ireland. This arrangement was made permanent in 1949 when the United Kingdom assured Northern Ireland that partition was part of the UK constitution.

During the 1950s and 1960s discrimination against Catholics was rife in Northern Ireland. Many were denied the opportunity to work or own property. The power to vote was also denied to many and therefore there was little likelihood that Catholics would have any significant representation in parliament.

*Civil rights*

In 1967 the Northern Civil Rights Association was founded to help combat these injustices. The following year, in October, the Civil Rights marchers clashed with the police in Derry. The RUC attacked many of the marchers with batons. There is no doubt that this led to the troubles of the following year when there were a series of bombings and deaths in Belfast. The British army was drafted into Northern Ireland in 1969 and has remained there to the present day. The bombings, shootings and killings have continued ever since and, despite occasional ceasefires, there does not seem any permanent solution on the horizon.

Much of Seamus Heaney's poetry refers to aspects of Irish history. The content of some poems can easily be related to specific incidents e.g. 'Requiem for the Croppies' (*Door into the Dark*) or 'Casualty' (*Field Work*) but in most poems the poet tends to look at the whole picture and draw universal conclusions or ask wide-ranging questions. The summaries and commentaries below discuss the relationship between poems and history much more specifically.

# PART TWO

# Summaries

## General summary

Seamus Heaney is one of the greatest living poets. We might feel that a poet who is held in such high regard should cause us great difficulty when we come to read his work but we find that this is not the case. Most of his poetry is straightforward. The poet speaks to us in a clear, direct manner.

Our task in this book will be to read and analyse some of the poetry from Seamus Heaney's earlier works, *Death of a Naturalist*, *Door into the Dark*, *Wintering Out*, *North* and *Field Work*.

**Death of a Naturalist:** *loss of childhood innocence*

The poetry in *Death of a Naturalist* examines the theme of death in the literal and **metaphorical** (see Literary Terms) sense. Seamus Heaney writes about the death of his infant brother but he also writes about the death of his childhood innocence. While this death creates great sadness for that which is left behind, it also creates a new found freedom. Freedom, however, also introduces fear and a loss of stability. Thus it is that from all of this turbulence Seamus Heaney begins to find his poetic voice. The two best-known poems in this first volume are 'Death of a Naturalist' and 'Mid-Term Break'. The title poem discusses the comfortable nature and fun of his early life and then suddenly we read about the loss of security and the terror felt by the young boy as he realises that he has stepped into a new, adult world. 'Mid-Term Break' is not only a poignant commemoration of his little brother's death but also an acceptance of his adult responsibilities, perhaps for the first time. The two poems are vital to the spirit of *Death of a Naturalist* and they help the reader to see the struggle inside the young poet.

**Door into the Dark: *a confident writer***

The second collection, *Door into the Dark*, shows the reader a more confident Seamus Heaney who is prepared to take risks and to explore new areas. The final poem in the first book, *Death of a Naturalist*, ends with the lines:

> I rhyme
> To see myself, to set the darkness echoing.

which tells us his reasons for writing poetry. He continues the theme of searching the darkness in *Door into the Dark*. He searches into the art of writing poetry, the darkness of his own self and also Irish history and the Irish countryside. The bloody battle of Vinegar Hill is told in ballad form and is linked closely to the land itself in 'Requiem for the Croppies'. Seamus Heaney says that he sees the bogland as 'the memory of the landscape' and in 'Bogland' he 'set up – or rather laid down – the bog as an answering Irish myth' (*Preoccupations*, Faber and Faber, 1980) – an answer to the myth of the West and the frontier to the American people.

**Wintering Out*: understanding the ordinary***

*Wintering Out* examines the unknown and the strange in an attempt to understand the ordinary. The poetry looks at the past as a means of understanding the present. 'The Tollund Man' is a poem which has a direct connection with the terrible events in Northern Ireland. The man himself is a symbol of the innocent victims of the gun and the bomb. Seamus Heaney says that when he saw the photographs of the corpses he was immediately reminded of the 'atrocities, past and present, in the long rites of Irish political and religious struggles' (*Preoccupations*, Faber and Faber, 1980). Most poems in the collection are poems of exploration, discovery and symbolism and therein lies their power.

**North:**
**Seamus**
**Heaney**
**confronts the**
**problems of**
**the North**

Seamus Heaney recognises that the collection *North* is the consolidation of all that has gone before. More than ever in this collection he faces up to his thoughts and feelings about the problems experienced in Northern Ireland. He feels that it is necessary to write directly in a way that will show the horror of the time and the fear it engendered. The poet was under intense pressure at this time to become a poet of the troubles, to become a more political 'voice'. Titles such as 'Funeral Rites', 'Whatever You Say Say Nothing', 'The Ministry of Fear' and 'A Constable Calls' give a clear indication of the flavour of the poetry.

**Field Work:**
**deaths of**
**friends and**
**relatives**

*Field Work* is a meditation on the poet's friends and relatives who have died. Some of his friends and relatives were killed by the bullet or blown up in a bomb blast and some were famous artists such as the great Irish composer, Sean O'Riada. Of course the meditation on these deaths leads to the wider questions about the Province itself, questions such as:

> How culpable was he
> That last night when he broke
> Our Tribe's complicity? ('Casualty')

in other words how responsible can the innocent be for their own deaths? He asks another question in 'After a Killing': 'Who's sorry for our trouble?'

It echoes the comforting cliché in 'Mid-Term Break' when the old men tell him they were sorry for his trouble. But now there is no comfort because we have to presume that there is no sorrow, only bitterness or indifference. The collection, however, is not only about death and the troubles. There are also poems on the themes of love, marriage and politics and there are also pastoral poems and, finally, a translation from Dante.

# Detailed Summaries

## Death of a Naturalist

### Digging

The poet accepts that he does not have the skill to till the land and instead is happy to use his pen instead of the spade.

He is writing in his room and underneath he hears his father's spade in the gravel. His father is an expert and his rhythmic movement shows the skill that he has inherited from the poet's grandfather.

Seamus Heaney's grandfather could cut more peat than any other man. He did not waste time resting. He continued to work without pause until, finally, he reached the quality peat.

The poet tells the reader that his own talents lie in a different direction – he feels more comfortable with a pen in his hand and he will explore his roots through his writing.

**Comment** In the first two lines the reader senses that Seamus Heaney is comfortable with his chosen profession but we also realise that there is a hint of danger. There is a hint of the troubles that are never far away in Northern

*Consider the father's talent and the poet's choice of profession.*

Ireland. The **onomatopoeia** (see Literary Terms) of 'rasping' and 'gravelly' help create the sound made by his father's spade. It is appropriate that he should be engaging in his skill while his son is occupied with his chosen talent. Now the father is seen digging among the flowerbeds and, when he rises, the memory of twenty years ago is evoked when the young poet remembers his father digging potatoes. The father's skill is shown in the 'rhythm' of his movement just as the poet deals in rhythm all his life. The precise nature of the skill is emphasised in the detail observed by the poet – 'The coarse boot nestled on the lug, the shaft / Against the inside knee was levered firmly' – and then the poet emphasises the awe in which he held his father's and his grandfather's talents in the following **couplet** (see Literary Terms): 'By God, the old man could handle a spade. / Just like his old man'.

The language and structure of the lines are of everyday language, as if he were talking to his friends expressing his pride in their skill. While acknowledging their skill, he also feels some guilt because he has not continued the family tradition of labouring in the fields. However he does make a strong case that he is faithful to his ancestry because he does comment on, examine and extract riches from the 'living roots' that 'awaken in my head'. In other words his poetry is extracted from and is a commentary on the life and land of his fathers.

GLOSSARY      **drills** rows of plants
                         **lug** lower part of the spade which juts out

## DEATH OF A NATURALIST

The poet speaks to us of the fear caused by nature seeking revenge on the writer as a young boy. He tells us of a vision of a foul-smelling pond created by rotting vegetation. The flies make a blanket of noise over the water. The young boy's delight when playing with frogspawn is obvious. He is collecting the jelly for his nature study lessons at school. Miss Walls teaches the children about the frog's reproduction process and also explains that frogs change colour with the weather.

The second half of the poem is a description of the fear felt by the child when he is convinced that the frogs have visited the pond to take revenge for the theft of the frogspawn. The poet describes the threatening movement and sound of the invaders. Finally he turns and runs from the fearful new world.

COMMENT

*Note the young boy's love of nature*

Seamus Heaney creates a very comfortable world in the first section of the poem. He actually enjoyed the festering 'flax-dam', and the rotting vegetation, the insects murmuring as they hovered overhead and 'best of all' the feel of the tadpoles. We can feel the pleasure of the young child who is totally in tune with nature. The poet uses words such as 'festered', 'rotted', 'sweltered', 'gargled delicately', 'thick slobber' and 'clotted water', to show a young boy who is happy to meet nature in all its unpleasantness. Miss Walls is a central part of this world and it is for her that he collects the frogspawn. The language and the construction create an image of an infant engrossed in a world created by the teacher. He repeats, self-importantly, the information passed on by the teacher. He repeats the infant phrases 'daddy frog' and 'mummy frog' and this helps to emphasise what a protected world he lives in.

*Then comes nature's revenge.*

In contrast to the first section the menace of the invading frogs terrifies the young boy. The **imagery** (see Literary Terms) builds the feeling that an attack is imminent. The first line 'Then one hot day ...' immediately gives the reader the impression that the atmosphere is about to change. Words and phrases such as 'angry frogs', 'invaded' and 'poised like mud grenades' help to emphasise the image of hostile attack. Seamus Heaney creates menacing sounds 'coarse croaking', 'thick with a bass chorus', 'slap and plop' and 'blunt heads farting' to show the threatening, overwhelming nature of the 'enemy' that has been created in the boy's imagination. He immediately feels 'sickened' by the images and he flees. The visions of the 'great slime kings' and of the clutching frogspawn are the stuff of vivid childish nightmares.

*How realistic is Seamus Heaney's exploration of the child's terror?*

Seamus Heaney is exploring the terror which is felt by the young boy when he moves from the protection of the known world to a world which has little comfort and of which he has little knowledge. It is a world of guilt and emotions that he finds very difficult to control. His first instinct is to run away but we are left with the question – where does he run to now that he has lost his childhood?

GLOSSARY     **flax** plant grown for making linen

## BLACKBERRY-PICKING

Seamus Heaney writes about picking blackberries as a child, the joy it gave him and, finally, the disappointment he felt when the fruit turned sour. He begins the poem with a simple statement about the time during which the blackberries ripened. He describes the sensual pleasure he received from the berries and also describes their visual impact. He and his fellow pickers filled all the containers they could find. Soon, however, their joy was dissipated when they discovered a foul fungus eating into their find and an unpleasant smell from the fruit-filled vessels. He felt like crying because of his blighted hopes. Each year, he

says, he hoped that the blackberries would retain their
beauty but in his heart he knew that he was deceiving
himself.

COMMENT

*Seamus Heaney*
*describes the*
*transitory nature*
*of instant*
*pleasure.*

Seamus Heaney's images, in the beginning, are very
sensual. He gives the reader a vision of a young boy
who experiences pleasure to the full only to feel towards
the end, the disappointment that the aftermath of
instant pleasure often brings. But even in the first
section Seamus Heaney hints that all is not well. The
nightmarish visions of 'Death of a Naturalist' are there
again when he speaks of 'big dark blobs' which 'burned
/ Like a plate of eyes' and also when he expresses his
guilt as if there was blood on his hands like those of
Bluebeard. However most of the first section is
imbued with unalloyed pleasure even 'lust' which
indicates the awakening of sexual excitement. Seamus
Heaney tells us that the 'flesh was sweet' and that he
had a 'lust for / Picking'. He also uses phrases such as
'glossy purple clot', 'thickened wine' and 'summer's
blood', all of which shows the heightened awareness of
the initiate.

The second section is filled with sadness. The sexual
pleasure does not last and when it dissipates he is left
with feelings of emptiness and despair. The nightmare
images continue. The poet tells the reader that they
found, 'A rat-grey fungus, glutting on our cache'. They
also discovered that 'The fruit fermented' and that the
'canfuls smelt of rot'. The phrase 'sweet flesh would
turn sour' conjures an image of a rotting carcass and
Seamus Heaney's secondary message about the
transitory nature of instant gratification. There is
pathos in the last line when we hear that the boy,
despite all the evidence to the contrary, hopes that the
pleasures will remain.

FOLLOWER

Seamus Heaney describes his father ploughing the field, controlling the horses with appropriate noises. He observes the technicalities that are necessary and expertly turns over the sod, turns the horses and creates straight furrows. The poet writes about his own involvement in the activity. He stumbled along behind his father who sometimes swung the young boy onto his shoulders as he guided the horses. Seamus Heaney mentions that it was his ambition then to be as fine a ploughman as his father but instead he was merely a 'nuisance', getting in the way and distracting his father by his constant chatter. Now, however, his father is the 'nuisance' and will not leave him alone.

COMMENT

*Observe the poet's relationship with his father.*

The first line is a statement of fact that his father was a ploughman who worked with horses. In the second line Seamus Heaney compares his father to an explorer, a pioneer and uses the **metaphor** (see Literary Terms) of the sailing ship moving with full power, silently about its business. His father is likewise silent except for his short, sharp commands to the horses. The father's skill and isolation is emphasised in the phrase 'An expert' which stands on its own without amplification. In the second and third **stanzas** (see Literary Terms) the poet emphasises the technique and the concentration required to complete a difficult task. The father's control over the horses is also noted first using 'his clicking tongue' and then 'a single pluck / Of reins'. The rhythm of his movement is observed in the last line of the fourth stanza 'Dipping and rising to his plod'. Despite the distraction of the boy on his shoulders the father's movement is as smooth as before.

In the last three stanzas Seamus Heaney tells us of his stumbling attempts to stay with his father and of his failed ambition to be an expert ploughman. Instead he

was always in the 'shadow' of his parent and the feeling
of failure is emphasised in the lines: 'I was a nuisance,
tripping, falling, / Yapping always'. He was alienated
from his father because of his ineptitude and because he
interfered with the serious work on the land.

Suddenly in the last few lines the situation is reversed
and in a bitter juxtaposition the son becomes the master
irritated by the 'stumbling' old man who 'will not go
away'. Now the splendid isolation of the 'expert' at the
beginning has been transformed into the isolation of
the useless and unwanted.

The last two lines create an image of the father's, and
therefore our own, ageing. The image is much more
pathetic than that of the child at the beginning because
of what has been and never will be again.

## MID-TERM BREAK

As a young boy Seamus Heaney sits in the college sick
bay waiting for his neighbours to collect him. At home
he meets his weeping father and also Jim Evans who
sympathises with him. He sees the baby laughing in its
cot and he is embarrassed when the adults shake him by
the hand. His mother shows her anger but cannot shed
any more tears. Later that evening the ambulance
carries the body home. The boy goes to the room where
the body is laid out among the snowdrops and candles.
He sees the bruises on his forehead but sees that the car
did not cause any other scars when the collision
occurred. Finally, we discover that the boy's dead
brother was only four years old when he died.

COMMENT

*Look at the way*
*family members cope*
*with the death.*

The thoughts of death are brought to the fore almost
immediately as the school bells remind the poet of the
church bells tolling for the funeral. The time is doom-
laden for the boy as he waits for the neighbours. In the
second **stanza** (see Literary Terms) we are aware that a

member of the family has died and that this tragedy is different because usually funerals did not disturb his father in the way that this one has. But still we do not know the full nature of the tragedy.

Seamus Heaney recalls the embarrassment felt by the teenage boy when the adults sympathise with him. The lines 'And Big Jim Evans saying it was a hard blow' and '… Old men standing up to shake my hand / And tell me they were "sorry for my trouble"' are conversational in tone and help to emphasise the intimate nature of the parish group who have gathered to console the family. However, in the midst of all this sadness, the baby is innocent of the tragedy as he laughs and plays in his pram. The boy hears the asides of the neighbours and we sense the alienation he feels apart from his mother's hand in his. His mother is trying to control her emotions but it is clear that she is outraged by what has happened. Unemotional though it appears to be, the statement about the ambulance arriving contains a world of emotion.

When the teenager visits the room the candles and the snowdrops appear to have softened the tragedy. The body has not been damaged apart from the poppy bruise. However the comparison of the coffin to the

cot brings us up short and prepares us for the shock
to come. And then comes the devastating last line
which, at last, contains all the bitterness felt by the
poet.

*Study the pathos*
*of the last lines.*
The many run-on lines and some colloquial language
give a conversational tone to the poem and enable the
poet to present an unemotional, terse description of the
event. Seamus Heaney allows the details to create the
pathos for the reader. He writes about his 'father
crying', 'Big Jim Evans saying it was a hard blow', 'old
men standing up to shake my hand' and his mother
coughing out 'angry tearless sighs'. Finally, the poem
explodes with the bombshell of a last line: 'A four foot
box, a foot for every year'.

## PERSONAL HELICON

The young boy found it impossible to resist the lure of
dark, deep wells. He loved to look down there and
discover the depths. In **stanza** (see Literary Terms) two
he describes the well in a brickyard that was so deep he
could not see his reflection. But in the next stanza he
does see his reflection when he removes the vegetation
from the shallow water under a ditch and there he can
see his face at the bottom. He liked the sound of the
echoes when he shouted into the well. It seemed like
music to him. Sometimes, however, he was frightened
and he describes an occasion when a rat ran across the
face of the well. Now, however, he feels that it is not
adult-like to explore wells or to look at his reflection
like Narcissus. Instead he now writes to find himself
and to 'set the darkness echoing'.

COMMENT
The word 'Helicon' in the title refers to the mountain
which was the habitat of the muses of Ancient
Greek mythology. The artists who drank the water
of the streams which flowed down its sides were given

the power to write poetry. Seamus Heaney is talking here about writing poetry – his poetry.

*Consider Seamus Heaney's reasons for writing poetry.* The literal meaning of the poem is about the exploring of wells but the **metaphorical** (see Literary Terms) meaning is the central theme. Seamus Heaney is writing a poem about the creative process and about how he hopes to explore the dark recesses of the mind. Sometimes, he says, the depths to be plumbed are so deep that he cannot see where his instincts are leading him – 'So deep you saw no reflection in it' – and there are other times when the reflection comes back clear and sudden. It is now we understand one of the poet's main themes, that one function of poetry is to help the poet to reveal himself to himself. This reflection is not without its risks because there are moments of fear when the poet discovers the darkness of himself that confronts him and unnerves him.

The final lines of the poem make a very definite statement. Seamus Heaney says that he will write poetry so that he may know himself more fully and also in order to explore the recesses that have been closed to him until now. This is the final poem in *Death of a Naturalist* and it leads neatly into the second collection *Door into the Dark*.

GLOSSARY      **Narcissus** a character from Greek myth who loved his own reflection

**A** *Identify the person or creature 'to whom' the following lines refer.*

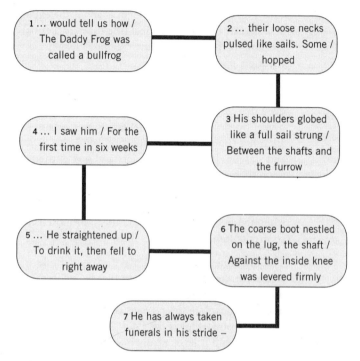

1 ... would tell us how / The Daddy Frog was called a bullfrog

2 ... their loose necks pulsed like sails. Some / hopped

3 His shoulders globed like a full sail strung / Between the shafts and the furrow

4 ... I saw him / For the first time in six weeks

5 ... He straightened up / To drink it, then fell to right away

6 The coarse boot nestled on the lug, the shaft / Against the inside knee was levered firmly

7 He has always taken funerals in his stride –

Check your answers on page 80.

**B** *Consider these issues.*

**a** Seamus Heaney's treatment of the loss of childhood.

**b** The poet's admiration for his father and grandfather.

**c** The reasons for writing poetry.

**d** The theme of exploration in poetry.

**e** The theme of loss in 'Mid-Term Break'.

## DOOR INTO THE DARK

### REQUIEM FOR THE CROPPIES

The poet narrates the story of part of the rebellion of 1798 (see Context and Setting). The narrator is one of the group of men who rebelled against the English. The men kept on the move through the fields, hiding when necessary, the priest and the tramp sharing the same ditch. It was not possible to plan ahead and strategy was decided on the run. They stampeded cattle into the foot soldiers and then attacked the cavalry from their positions in the hedges. But all was in vain. On Vinegar Hill the rebels were defeated and thousands met their deaths because they were ill-equipped. Their picks and scythes were no match for the cannons of the enemy. They were buried without ceremony and later that year the barley that they had in their pockets for food took root and grew into a harvest crop.

COMMENT    The story is narrated in the style of a folk tale because Seamus Heaney is here attempting to communicate with ordinary people of the soil. The rhyme scheme is simple and straightforward in the style of the ballads which commemorated all the great battles in Ireland's history. The last five lines of the poem are a lament for all those who gave their lives:

> Until, on Vinegar Hill, the fatal conclave.
> Terraced thousands died, shaking scythes at cannon.
> The hillside blushed, soaked in our broken wave.
> They buried us without shroud or coffin
> And in August the barley grew up out of the grave.

*How did Vinegar Hill contain the seeds of revolution?*

The final line suggests that the defiance of Vinegar Hill is the seed for future insurrection. Seamus Heaney is here clearly showing his support for the nationalist cause. He wrote this poem on the anniversary of the 1916 uprising and he later wrote, 'I did not realise at the time that the original heraldic murderous encounter between Protestant yeomen and Catholic rebel was to be initiated again in the summer of 1969, in Belfast, two months after *Door into the Dark* was published' (*Preoccupations*, Faber and Faber, 1980). The poet recognised the cyclical nature of Irish history and of the Irish Troubles in particular.

GLOSSARY    **Croppies**  the 'croppy boys', who were so called because they cut their hair in the style of the peasants of the Industrial Revolution
**Vinegar Hill**  see Context and Setting

## BOGLAND

The poet writes of the broad expanse of the prairies which does not hinder the eye and compares it to the narrowing of our focus when we observe the bogland, the bogland which has no fences. The turf dries to a hard crust under the baking sun. The skeleton of the Great Irish Elk was preserved in the peat of the bog and has now been removed and set up elsewhere where its huge antlers are on show. Butter has been preserved in the bog for more than one hundred years and the ground is like butter as it gives way underfoot. The rotting vegetation will never create coal and the turfcutters will only hit the soft trunks of trees as they dig downwards for the turf. The poet feels that the bogholes are so deep that the water might have seeped underneath the peat from the Atlantic seepage.

COMMENT

*Consider the way Seamus Heaney compares those who dig in the bog to those who discover heritage.*

The poem refers to the many rather than to individuals. The many include the people of Ireland's past, the people of Ireland's present and also the people of Ireland's future. The treasures of the past are yielded up to the present and will influence the future. The bogland is the framework which preserves the past history and past treasures and allows continuity into the present and into the future.

The poet compares the wide vision that the prairie allows and the focussed, concentrated vision that the bogland demands. The 'horizon' narrows the vision and forces the poet and the reader to look closely at that which has been preserved from the past. The Great Irish Elk and the butter are **metaphors** (see Literary Terms) for the whole of the Irish heritage and the great treasures that we must search for in '… black butter / Melting and opening underfoot'.

*The land invites us to explore the past.*

The ground, Seamus Heaney says, is soft and inviting – the past calling to us to dig up its contents that will enrich our future. He tells us that the 'ground itself is kind, black butter'. The land is 'kind' in the sense that it looks after people, but it is also 'kind' in the sense that it allows us to enter its hidden chambers to discover the limitless bounty from the past.

In the last two **stanzas** (see Literary Terms) the poet writes of the 'pioneers' who dig downwards and find layer upon layer of history, mythology and folklore. The pioneers are those who search for and find the Irish heritage and the bog is the metaphorical repository, and sometimes actual repository, of this heritage. He tells us finally, that 'The wet centre is bottomless' and this implies that the search is endless and that while the 'pioneers' go on looking they will find more and more that is valuable.

ANAHORISH

This is one of Seamus Heaney's place name poems. Anahorish is a townland, one of the areas in a local parish. The full name is 'Anach fhior uisce' which means 'the place of clear water', a phrase that occurs in the first line of the poem.

The poem begins with the spring wells gushing from the hill and onto the grass and cobbles. The poet speaks of the gentle, sloping lane and compares the gentle sounds of the word 'Anahorish' to the soft gradient. He remembers the winter evenings lit by the oil lamps of the farmers as they walked through the farmyards. The poet tells us that they are like the original inhabitants of the hill as they walk through the mist to break the ice of wells and dunghills.

COMMENT

*How does the poet evoke history?*

The sound of the word 'Anahorish' is all important in this poem. Throughout he feels secure, comfortable in his environment and the softness of the vowels and the consonants help to emphasise this security. Seamus Heaney is almost obsessed with his 'sense of place' and this poem is typical of his exploration. This townland is his place, part of his home and while writing about the area he takes the opportunity to explore his historical roots. They are obscured by the mists of time but, nevertheless, he sees the farmworkers as direct descendants of those who inhabited the hill in ancient times.

The phrase '... mound dwellers / go waist-deep in mist' is evocative of Celtic mythology and of a time when Ireland was yet to be violated by successive hostile invasions. This concept connects nicely with 'My "place of clear water" / the first hill in the world' at the beginning. This was a place and a hill unpopulated by time or enemies. The phrase 'first hill in the world' is, in one sense, childlike in its construction but it also creates an image of the vastness and emptiness of pre-history.

WINTERING OUT

THE TOLLUND MAN

The poet thinks about one day going to see the Iron Age man in Aarhus in Denmark. He describes the

figure as he sees him in a photograph and he wants to
see him in reality. Details such as seeds from the man's
final meal remaining in his stomach, his nakedness and
the noose and belt that helped tie him down are noted
by the poet and he promises that he will stand there
observing him for 'a long time'. The man has been
sacrificed to the goddess of fertility and has been
preserved in the dark liquids of the bog. From there he
was removed to Aarhus.

Seamus Heaney feels that he could, blasphemously,
pray to the Tollund Man to bring back to earth the four
brothers who were ambushed, killed and buried in the
farmyards of Ireland. As he continues his journey he
knows that he will feel some of the sadness felt by this
man. As he passes through the areas he will recite their
names and he will watch the country people pointing at
him as they once did to the Tollund Man and he will
not understand their language. Now he feels a sadness
at the familiar feeling that comes over him – of the
killing fields of his own country.

COMMENT

*Note the
connections
between pagan
sacrifice, Catholic
ritual and
nationalism.*

This poem is from the collection *Wintering Out* (1972)
which contains many poems about the bog people.
Seamus Heaney sees connections between the sacrifice
of the Tollund Man and the 'executions' in Northern
Ireland.

In the opening two **stanzas** (see Literary Terms)
Seamus Heaney creates an image of a man who is
wedded to the earth and to nature. He mentions his
'peat-brown head', 'the mild pods of his eyelids' and
writes about 'gruel of winter seeds' which are 'Caked in
his stomach'. There is an emphasis here on the union of
the sacrificed priests (of whom the Tollund Man was
almost certainly one) to the goddess of fertility. The
link between pagan worship of the goddess and Seamus
Heaney's own Catholic liturgy is clear in the third verse
when he says: 'I will stand a long time' reminding the

reader of the worshipful stance of the faithful before the cross and later, in the second section, when he prays (despite the risk of blasphemy), to the Tollund Man to resurrect the bodies of the four brothers who were sacrificed for somebody's beliefs. So here we have three layers flowing into each other and each influencing the other. The fate of the Tollund Man represents pagan sacrifice, Seamus Heaney's own Catholic ritual and, finally, the sacrifice of the victims by the modern men of violence on the altar of nationalism.

## WEDDING DAY

Wedding Day is a personal poem about the uncertainty that partners feel as they set out on married life. The narrator talks about the fearful images that flash through his mind. He cannot understand the sadness that is welling up all around on this day. He paints a picture of 'a deserted bride' who hides behind the cake and 'goes through the ritual' in spite of doubts and sorrow. At last he finds some comfort when he goes to the gents and sees a heart pierced with an arrow and remembers that the wedding, is, in the end, about love.

### COMMENT

*Study the contradictory feelings.*

The poem begins abruptly with the comment, 'I am afraid'. The poet creates the feeling of a silent horror film showing us image after image of groom, bridegroom and guests filled with sadness. The groom is unbalanced and cannot understand the 'wild grief'. The picture of the bride is superimposed with the image of Miss Havisham (from Charles Dickens's *Great Expectations*) who was deserted by her husband to be. The tension of the poem is created when the poet confronts the reader with the contradictory messages that are part of the wedding day, the joy and sadness, love and loss, security and uncertainty. Phrases such as 'Sound has stopped', 'wild grief', 'a deserted bride', 'Who persists demented' and 'skewered heart' help create the feeling of disorientation and edginess. But then, finally, he is calmed by the expectation of a quiet journey to the airport with his love. He dismisses all the sorrow and uncertainty when he asks: '… Let me / Sleep on your breast to the airport'.

## WESTERING

Seamus Heaney wrote this poem while he was in California and he remembers his journey from Ireland to America. He sits under Rand McNally's map of the moon and its craters remind him of frogskin. He recalls his last night in Donegal before he set out for America. The moonlight casts his shadow on the white-washed wall in the farmyard and he sees the objects as all bone and egg, surreal as the image of the moon itself. Their journey begins on Good Friday while all parishioners are at church and this gives the area a strange sense of peace. He hears the clappers which on this day have been substituted for the usual bell and he imagines the congregations in all the churches paying homage to the crucified Christ. The moon shows the wounds of Christ and he imagines the Body of Christ loosened on the cross because of his blasphemy when he travelled on Good Friday.

### COMMENT

*How does the image of Christ influence Seamus Heaney's thoughts?*

The discovery made by the poet is not that of a new world but, instead, he discovers a new way of looking at his own world back in Donegal. He is also forced to study himself and the way he behaves.

Seamus Heaney's journey to America is similar to a journey to the moon. His movement away from the Church arouses pangs of guilt but also creates a lightness within him. Words such as 'free fall', 'empty amphitheatre', 'dwindling', 'Falling' and 'loosening' suggest the feeling of freedom that he experiences as he moves further away from the constraints of the church.

The freestyle that Seamus Heaney encountered in America is evident in this poem and this relaxed framework helps to create the unhurried nature of his long, winding journey.

The final two **stanzas** (see Literary Terms) evoke the image of a troubled poet standing far back and studying the troubles of the North. He is 'Six thousand miles away' from his war-torn homeland and he contemplates the 'untroubled dust' of the moon unlike the chaos in Ulster. The final couplet gives us Christ 'weighing', perhaps judging the actions of those past and present in the province and it also asks us to consider Christ himself, hanging on the cross.

**A** *Identify the person or persons 'to whom' these comments refer.*

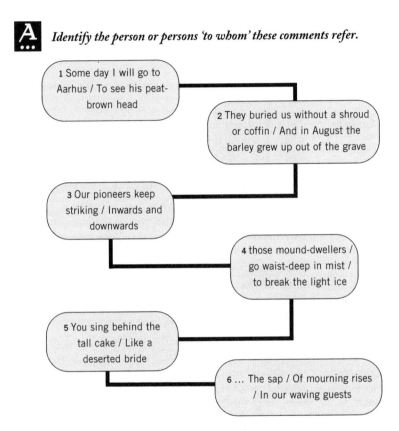

1 Some day I will go to Aarhus / To see his peat-brown head

2 They buried us without a shroud or coffin / And in August the barley grew up out of the grave

3 Our pioneers keep striking / Inwards and downwards

4 those mound-dwellers / go waist-deep in mist / to break the light ice

5 You sing behind the tall cake / Like a deserted bride

6 ... The sap / Of mourning rises / In our waving guests

Check your answers on page 80.

**B** *Consider these issues.*

a The importance of Irish history in Seamus Heaney's poetry.

b Seamus Heaney's 'sense of place'.

c The link between past troubles and present violence.

d The contradictory nature of marriage.

e Seamus Heaney's antipathy to catholicism.

## NORTH

### MOSSBAWN: TWO POEMS IN DEDICATION

Both poems are written in dedication to Mary Heaney, the poet's aunt.

*1. Sunlight*  The poet describes the farmyard outside the kitchen where a woman is baking. All is quiet as the sun shines and heats the water pump. The reflection of the sun causes the water to look like honey. In the afternoon the splash of sunlight on the wall looks like the baking iron which has been left outside. Inside, the woman is warmed by the oven as she busies herself with her baking. In her floury apron she dusts the board with a feather and her nails are white from the flour. Again, all is quiet as the poet hears the ticking of the clocks. He feels that the love of the afternoon is as concrete as the tin scoop which is buried in the meal-bin.

COMMENT

*Note the tranquil nature of farmhouse life.*

The poem evokes peace and calm, a timeless space where all is unhurried. The first nine lines create images of light and heat in the farmyard, friendly warm pictures in the mind, all of which help to create a framework for the homely scene of his aunt baking within. The word 'absence' in the phrase 'sunlit absence' has a positive quality creating a link with the idea of 'space' in the penultimate **stanza** (see Literary Terms). These words do not imply negative emptiness, but instead suggest places where one can be refreshed and able to think and to be oneself.

*Look at the precise nature of Seamus Heaney's imagery.*

The actions of his aunt are drawn with precision. We see images of her 'hands', of the 'bakeboard', the 'reddening stove', her 'floury apron', her 'whitened nails' and many more. All these images are of an ordinary country woman going about her unhurried life, without stress or worry, of a woman who is full of

love for those she cares for as the poet says in the final
four lines:

> And here is love
> like a tin smith's scoop
> Sunk past its gleam
> in the meal-bin.

The picture of tranquillity created here is in contrast to
the frenetic pace of life in other parts of Northern
*Contrast farmhouse* Ireland, in contrast to the bombs and guns and in
*life with the* contrast to the threats and posturings of politicians and
*violence in* terrorists. Yet this love and peace is firmly rooted in
*Northern Ireland.* reality, in the day-to-day activities of the ordinary
people.

**2. The Seed** The poet calls on Jan Breughel, a sixteenth-century
**Cutters** painter, to help him create images of the 'seed cutters'
in the mind of the reader. We see them as beings from
a bygone age. They kneel in a semi-circle, protecting
themselves from the wind, while they halve the seed
potatoes. The leaves that grow from the seed potatoes
are seen above the ground while the potatoes
themselves are buried under the protection of the straw.
As in 'Sunlight' the poet creates an image of people
working without hurry, They cut open each potato to
discover a watermark at the centre. The poet asks that
the seasonal traditions continue and he suggests that
the painter compose a painting which will emphasise
the importance of the group even though each
individual will live out an anonymous life.

COMMENT The opening statement places the seed cutters back in
history, perhaps in the time of Breughel himself or even
before. Seamus Heaney derives deep satisfaction from
the fact that a task such as theirs should continue
through the ages until his own time. He emphasises
their significance when he says boldly, 'They are the
seed cutters'. The images are sharp and precise just as in

*Examine the poet's plea for unity.*

'Sunlight'. They are images that have been created through the centuries without a break. The ritual activities are quiet and peaceful and offer an escape from a war-torn province. The poet pleads that these traditions may continue and his final request is that there may be unity and he wants the painter to compose the frieze which will portray everybody without any distinctive labels.

## FUNERAL RITES

In this poem Seamus Heaney is desperately searching for a satisfactory burial for those who have been killed in the violence of Northern Ireland and also more significantly an end to the cycle of murder and mayhem.

The poet sees his shouldering of the coffin as a 'kind of manhood', a taking on of some adult responsibility.

The relations who have died are laid out in the customary manner so that friends and relatives pay their last respects to the dead. Seamus Heaney describes in great detail the faces and hands of the deceased. The fingers are criss-crossed with rosary beads and the wrists have been arranged to form the hands in an attitude of prayer. The poet admires the whole picture, the candle-lit scene, the woman waiting respectfully and the crucifixes on the coffin. The lid is nailed down and the funeral procession begins.

*Yet another appeal for one nation in Ireland.*

In the second section there is a cry for a funeral ceremony that will reconcile the community. The poet wishes that there should be one great burial site in the centre of Ireland for all those killed. He asks that this burial site should be in 'the great chambers of Boyne' giving the grave the dignity of tradition. Then the nation (not just Catholics) would take part in the procession. The women left behind would celebrate the great coming together by imagining the 'slow triumph'. He compares the procession to a snake whose tail moves from the North just as the head enters the tomb.

When the bodies have been buried the mourners will drive back to the North and this time there will be no talk of revenge only the memory of 'those under the hill'. The poet remembers the burial of Gunnar, a Norse hero, who was killed violently and yet there was no attempt made to avenge his death. It was said that four lights burned in the corner of his burial chamber and he himself sang about honour and when the chamber opened up he looked joyfully at the moon.

COMMENT    Seamus Heaney is detached at the beginning of the poem. He observes carefully the comforting ritual of the ceremony and he shows respect for the dead but he cannot feel any more than that. He says that he: '… knelt courteously / admiring it all'.

He notices that the hands are 'shackled' and that the wrists are 'obediently sloped'. But then he suddenly becomes involved as he notices the 'Dear soapstone masks' and as he kisses the 'igloo brows' before the coffins are closed forever.

*Study the poet's concept of the united funeral procession.*

In section two the poet muses on 'each neighbourly murder'. The phrase suggests that the killings are always close to home and are, therefore, all the more evil for that. There is a desperate need for ceremony and ritual. The poet feels that 'each blinded home' is prepared to ignore the possibilities of reconciliation. He, on the other hand, wished to see the dead buried in the centre of Ireland. He wants the funeral procession to be a 'slow triumph' of a nation coming together and forgetting its past. The drums are 'muffled' because these are the drums of peace not the drums of war: 'the whole country tunes / to the muffled drumming / of ten thousand engines'.

*Seamus Heaney
suggests that the
country might be
better reverting to
paganism.*

Seamus Heaney believes that this pagan ceremony
should be revived because it would take the country
back to its traditional roots and there would not be any
possibility of religious strife in the ritual itself. The
image of the snake is significant. St Patrick banished
the snake from Ireland's shores and now the poet recalls
the serpent to reinforce his concept of a traditional
pagan ceremony.

In the final section the mourners gain comfort from
'imagining those under the hill'. No longer will the long
journey home be filled with thoughts of violence and
revenge.

The images of the procession passing 'Strang' and
'Carling fjords' lead us to a meditation on the beautiful
death and burial in Njals saga. Seamus Heaney evokes
the Viking past of Ireland and in this Norse Saga we
are reminded of the unavenged death of Gunnar which
broke the cycle of vengeance and feuds. His message is
clear. If the Viking culture with its code of vengeance is
capable of creating such a noble saga perhaps we should
turn to our pagan past for ceremony and not continue
with our Catholic and Protestant rituals.

## NORTH

The poet sees himself as someone searching for
answers, not by questioning his own spirit, but by
looking to the world further afield.

When the poet returns to the Atlantic he faces Iceland
and Greenland but it is not until his imagination is
touched by the Vikings that his soul is stirred. He
examines their violent achievements and he is warned
by their voices and actions from the past. He is urged to
'lie down / in the word–hoard' and to 'Compose in
darkness'. He must not expect continued flashes of
insight but instead light spread thinly over his own

familiar thoughts. The actions of the warlike warriors will not in themselves create his art but his movement into their world will help him to make sense of his own world in the North.

COMMENT     The poem studies the brutal realities that caused the Viking atrocities and attempts to create something constructive from the experience. The poet's relationship with the Viking ghosts is so intimate that he can listen to their advice and heed their warnings. He hears, from the depths of the longships, their cries against violence. He realises that even now, all these years later, we cannot but be touched by the actions of the Norsemen.

The poet is unaffected by the blandness of Iceland and by 'the pathetic colonies / of Greenland' but he is shaken by the 'fabulous raiders' who speak to him through 'longship's swimming tongue'. They are backed and supported by the hindsight of history and tell the poet that the only peace they had was that which came from exhaustions after battle, after coarse sex, after vengeance and hatreds. And while they drew breath the 'spilled blood' was remembered and soon the process was reborn.

*The poet realises the difficulties when attempting to search for and express ideas.*

The longship's tongue tells the poet to enclose himself in the shadows of the 'word-hoard' and sift through all these imaginings until he is able to 'Compose in darkness' but he must not expect a continuous 'cascade of light' but rather the long, hard search for a glimmer here and there. He must trust his own imaginings and beliefs when writing. He is told:

> Keep your eye clear
> as the bleb of the icicle,
> trust the feel of what nubbed treasure
> your hands have known.

GLOSSARY    **althing** two meanings, either the ancient word meaning
'everything', or the title of the parliament of Iceland

## VIKING DUBLIN: TRIAL PIECES

Seamus Heaney writes yet another poem that links
Ireland to the Viking past. The poem begins with a
description of a drawing on a piece of bone which is
part of a Viking exhibition in Dublin. In part two he
muses on what he considers to be a learning process
and he compares it to his own craft of writing. When
the drawing is magnified for the on-looker it takes on a
shape that has a much greater significance, a Viking
boat rising and dipping through the Liffey. Part three
continues the exploration of the drawing and of his own
writing process.

*The poet sees*
*corruption all*
*around him.*

There is a dramatic change of direction in the fourth
and fifth sections. Seamus Heaney's subject is still
writing but now he makes it clear that he is so involved
with death and corruption that the 'rot / in the state'
becomes part of him and he, himself, is 'infused / with
its poisons'. The poet remembers the killings on both
sides as if they were scores in a 'neighbourly' football
match.

The poem is rounded off by Jimmy Farrell who,
conversationally, talks of the many skulls that can be
seen in the city. And Seamus Heaney is again,
grotesquely, hunting out death and corruption.

COMMENT     The poem concentrates on the writing process and the
poet again uses the connection between Ireland's
present and the country's Viking past to emphasise his
fascination with the troubled province.

In the first part there are repeated references to the
child's handwriting and this slides gently into the
second **stanza** (see Literary Terms) where the poet

compares his own 'trial pieces' with those of the
child. It is not until his writing has become 'magnified'
in his mind that he can see the larger picture, can see
where the poem is leading him. In section three the
poet delves further into his own craft and there is a
sense that he finds a ghoulish satisfaction in his
exploration:

> And now we reach in
> for shards of the vertebrae,
> the ribs of hurdle,
> the mother-wet caches –

The poet compares himself to Hamlet, the Prince of
Denmark, because he is too involved in death and its
causes and he is also poisoned by the very 'rot' that he is

*The poet worries
that he himself has
been corrupted.*

investigating. The fifth stanza brings us abruptly to the
present troubles in the North and we hear again of the
'neighbourly' killings and the tally of murders scrawled
on the walls.

The 'Jimmy Farrell' of the last section is a character
from *The Playboy of the Western World* (J.M. Synge,
Heinemann, 1991 – first published 1907) and he takes
us back to the National Museum of Dublin. He tells
his audience of the variety of skulls that are to be found
in the city and we are lead to the final numbing lines
when the poet creates an image of overwhelming
death:

> My words lick around
> cobbled quays, go hunting
> lightly as pampooties
> over the skull-capped ground.

## BONE DREAMS

The stimulus for the imagination is once again a piece
of bone but this time there are no drawings. He picks it
up and, **metaphorically** (see Literary Terms), throws it

towards England and his thoughts move backwards in time through the literary forms that have, over the centuries, influenced Irish culture. He examines the language and art forms of the forces which have invaded Ireland, the English, the Normans and indeed the Catholic Church itself.

*Study the poet's feelings about English Literature.*

The contradictory nature of Seamus Heaney's feelings towards England are explored in sections four and five. He intertwines love, landscape and literature to create the notion of a rich, erotic love affair that, nevertheless, entraps his mind.

The final image of the dead mole found in Devon is a metaphor for Seamus Heaney's emotions. Like himself the mole digs and like much of the literature it is dead and cold. In the end, however, he shows his affection for the country whose language and literature are part of himself.

COMMENT

The poem asks us to study the interaction between object and language. He sees the language and literature as being 'dead as stone' at first but touches it again only to find a valuable 'nugget'. Aggressively he picks up the bone and throws it at England using his 'sling of mind'. His literal action of throwing the bone at England expresses his anger that has come from years of frustration but he is also fascinated by the 'strange fields' that he feels bound to explore.

In the second section the poet enters the 'Bone-house' of the mind and discovers the skeletons of the languages and literatures that have imbued Irish art throughout the centuries. These cultures have always been visited upon Ireland at a price and that price has been the conquest of the nation by yet another invading force. And then he travels further back and finds the ancient word '*bān-hūs*' and in this place the spirit comes alive for a while:

> I found *bān-hūs*,
>
> its fire, benches,
> wattle and rafters,
> where the soul
> fluttered a while
>
> in the roofspace.

Seamus Heaney's love affair with the landscape and with language is powerfully evoked in sections four and five. He becomes the object of his love. He is changed *The poet actually* into bone and then into stone. The image changes *becomes the* again as he describes, erotically, his hands feeling *landscape that he* 'towards the passes'. He plays, sensuously, moving *describes.* between images. One moment he is the landscape and the next he is the observer and then the two are lovers enjoying one another completely:

> And we end up
> cradling each other
> between the lips
> of an earthwork.

The final section looks again at the contradictory nature of his feelings for the English nation and the English language. As he feels the dead mole's shoulders he remembers, lovingly, the Pennines and therefore the country with which he has such a strange relationship.

## BOG QUEEN

The narrator in this poem is the Bog Queen of Moira, a body discovered in a bog near Belfast in the eighteenth century. The woman was a Viking and so, again, the poet discovers the link between Ulster and the Province's Viking past. This is very important to Seamus Heaney because he now has physical, historical evidence to connect Northern Ireland with the Danish Vikings and Jutland itself.

The queen lies in the bogs waiting through the years to be discovered. In the meantime the body decays and becomes part of the bog itself. The 'queen' narrates in great detail the process of decay and tells how she became united with the landscape and she speaks for the whole earth: 'dawn suns groped over my head / and cooled at my feet'.

The incarceration is likened to a hibernation during the winter's cold and her discovery is compared to a rebirth.

COMMENT

*Study the symbolism of the Bog Queen.*

The poet has discovered a real connection between the Viking culture and the culture of Ireland's past.

The Bog Queen is a symbol for Ireland itself (Mother Ireland) and she speaks of the way she has been pillaged through the centuries: 'My skull hibernated / in the wet nest of my hair. / Which they robbed'.

She is also a symbol for the revolutionary movement which, by its very nature, had to remain under cover until ready to attack. The pain and resentment of the nationalists is expressed in terms of impatient waiting:

'I lay waiting

on the gravel bottom,
my brain darkening,
a far of spawn
fermenting underground

There is a feeling of coldness all through the poem and this links again with the icy Viking North. She tells us: 'through my fabrics and skins / the seeps of winter / digested me', and later we hear: 'I knew the winter cold / like the nuzzle of fjords at my thighs –'. The 'nuzzle of fjords' is a significant phrase because it ties the corpse to Ireland's Viking past of the North.

The final four **stanzas** (see Literary Terms) develop the concept of rebellion in two ways. In the first abortive attempt the rebel attempts to rise up but is soon suppressed by the authorities:

I was barbered
and stripped
by a turfcutter's spade

who veiled me again
and packed coomb softly
between the stone jambs
at my head and my feet.

However, the final monster rising from the grave of centuries of invasion and oppression is captured in the following lines:

The plait of my hair,
a slimy birth-chord
of bog, had been cut

and I rose from the dark,
hacked bone, skull-ware,
frayed stitches, tufts,
small gleams on the bank.

## PUNISHMENT

*Look at how
punishments of the
past are linked to
present revenge.*

Seamus Heaney studies another body exhumed from the bog and the manner of the death leads him to consider the punishments that have occurred and are occurring in Northern Ireland.

He can feel the objects used to execute and he can feel the rope around his neck as if he were the girl. The wind hardens her naked nipples and shivers her thin frame. He imagines her body immersed in the bog, weighed down by stone. The poet sees the body as part of the earth and of the vegetation. He speaks to the 'Little adultress' and tells her she was beautiful but, in

spite of his attraction, he knows that he too would have
let her die because he would have been afraid to speak
out. He accepts that he is a 'voyeur' of the inner parts of
her naked body. He knows he would have stayed quiet
then because he stands 'dumb' now when the girls of
his neighbourhood are 'tarred' and tied to the railings
because of their friendship with British soldiers.
Publicly he deplores the act but, privately, he knows
that he understands and accepts the reasons for
'intimate revenge'.

COMMENT     The poet is attracted to the body that he knows existed
before the stoning. He is as one with the body and feels
the suffering that the girl felt. He feels the rope
tightening and the wind whipping her nakedness. He
moves away in the third **stanza** (see Literary Terms)
and observes the heaviness of her body in the bog as it
sinks into the earth to become part of her burial
ground:

> Under which at first
> she was a barked sapling
> that is dug up
> oak-brain, brain-firkin
>
> her shaved head
> like a stubble of black corn

He regards her tenderly and writes of her 'memories of
love' and endearingly calls her 'Little adultress'.
Pityingly he almost whispers: 'My poor scapegoat, / I
almost love you', but straight away condemns himself –

*The poet confronts*     'but would have cast, I know, / the stones of silence',
*his own 'cowardice'*     thereby linking this condemnation with the reality of
*in the face of*         his cowardice in the present day violence:
*present-day*
*violence.*
> I who have stood dumb
> when your betraying sisters,
> cauled in tar,
> wept by the railings

The man who stands there deriving sexual pleasure from his observation of the dead body and from his recreation of her body in his imagination must accept that he himself is part of the punishment process. At the beginning he was as one with the punished girl – now he is as one with his own tribe, all of whom pretend in a show of 'civilised outrage' but deep inside fully sympathise with the need to punish those who betray the 'cause'.

## FROM 'WHATEVER YOU SAY SAY NOTHING'

The poem begins with an account of a meeting between the poet and an English journalist. The journalist wants to know more about the problems in Northern Ireland. The lines that follow are a collection of phrases that appear constantly in the media and are spoken by politicians on both sides. The neighbours are also guilty of cliché after cliché.

*Discrimination is still very prevalent in Northern Ireland.*

Part three expresses the frustration the poet feels with all of this 'Northern reticence'. He would like to break through this safe barrier. Underneath all of this, discrimination is still rife and a man's religion is signalled by his name.

That morning he had driven past the internment camp at Long Kesh which was set up to imprison, without trial, those who were arrested in 1971. It reminded him of the film of Stalag 17.

The witty phrase daubed on a wall in Ballymurphy assumes significance for the poet as he thinks about the miserable existence that many have in the province.

COMMENT

Seamus Heaney shows his frustration with the empty phrases not only of the media and politicians but also those used by himself and his neighbours. He is happier to use his rosary beads rather than to take seriously:

... the jottings and analyses
Of politicians and newspapermen
Who've scribbled down the long campaign from gas
And protest to gelignite and sten

But he and his fellow Irishmen realise that the way they
use language is very important if they hope to survive.
The admonition which gives its name to the poem
'Whatever you say, say nothing' is a summary of all the
stock phrases that are used by journalists and
inhabitants:

'Oh, it's disgraceful, surely, I agree.'
'Where's it going to end?' 'It's getting worse.'
'They're murderers.' 'Internment, understandably ...'
The 'voice of sanity' is getting hoarse.

The frustration continues to be expressed in section
three (section two has not been included in the *New
Selected Poems*) and he feels it is now about time that
the Dutchman's (King William of Orange – see
Context and Setting) influences begin to wane. He uses
his own name to generalise the Catholic population and
its persecution down the centuries – '... the dangerous
tide that followed Seamus'. But his frustration
continues, this time with himself because he is
'incapable' of writing poetry that will have any effect on
*The poet shows his*  the troubled province. He writes about the names that
*frustration because*  place people on one side of the divide or the other – '...
*of his inability to*  Sidney signalled Prod / And Seamus (call me Sean) was
*influence matters*  sure-fire Pape' – names that fuel the unrest just as
*in Northern*  surely as the unresolved feud between the sides. He
*Ireland.*  compares the Catholics in Northern Ireland to the
Greeks inside the 'wooden horse'. He says that they are
'Besieged within the siege'.

The final scene is viewed from the security of his car.
Outside he observes an alien countryside with a bomb
crater, an internment camp, machine guns and a

stockade, all of which remind him of a film he once saw
about Stalag 17. In one sense it is alien yet in another it
is all too familiar, all part of the anguished tapestry of
his country:

> Is there life before death? That's chalked up
> In Ballymurphy. Competence with pain,
> Coherent miseries, a bite and sup,
> We hug our little destiny again.

## From 'singing school'

*1. The
Ministry of
Fear*

The poet met Seamus Deane, to whom the poem is
dedicated, while he was at St Columb's School in
Derry. He describes the new vistas opened to him while
he looked out, desperately homesick. His mention of ·
local names such as Brandywell, Bogside and Lecky
Road help to establish the area in the reader's
imagination. He was so unhappy during his first week
at school that he could not eat his biscuits and threw
them over the fence.

*Seamus Heaney
acknowledges the
value of his
relationship with
Seamus Deane.*

Seamus Heaney remembers leaving to go to Queen's
University in Belfast and then on to Berkeley University
in California. During his time at school and at
university, he and Seamus Deane sent volumes of
poetry to one another. Seamus Heaney was puzzled by
the words and concepts in his friend's verses. He writes
about his accent as sounding very heavy and
cumbersome when mixed with the fine 'elocution' of
other academics. He ponders on the possibility that his
accent has changed and is reminded that it was often
suggested that Catholics did not speak as well as
Protestants. This 'stuff' led to a lack of confidence.
When he wrote home from school he kept up a
pretence that boarding school was 'not so bad'.

During the holidays the awkward couplings 'In the
kissing seat of an Austin Sixteen' soon gave way to the

dwindling evenings of freedom, but not before
altercations with the RUC. A gun was always pointed
at his head as the police gathered round the car. When
he gave his name the reaction was hostile. At one such
meeting the police read a poem by Seamus Deane but
they could not understand it. He makes the point that
Ulster does not have exclusive rights to English poetry.
The Catholics in Northern Ireland are surrounded by a
framework of fear.

COMMENT

*The discomfort experienced at school is realistically described.*

In 'The Ministry of Fear', Seamus Heaney sees the
education that he received at school as an uncivilised
and uncomfortable experience. The poet writes about
the uncertainty of growing up in Northern Ireland and
the brutalising experience of meeting the police when
he was a teenager.

The first section emphasises the unpleasant nature of
his time at boarding school. The vocabulary is loaded
with alien images e.g. 'lonely scarp', 'billeted / For six
years', 'inflamed throat', 'exile' and 'act / Of stealth'. He
writes that he 'gazed into new worlds' which further
increased his homesickness.

*Note the intimate nature of the writers' relationship.*

His life moved on to the next stage when he began to
grow as an artist and he was able to take comfort from
the friendship and support of Seamus Deane. There is
an intimacy in the way he writes about the friendship
that creates an image of a union dedicated to writing.
They are also united in their memory of comments
made to create feelings of inferiority, comments such as
'... Catholics, in general, don't speak / As well as
students from the Protestant schools'. He returns to his
memory of school and his guilt at not revealing the true
nature of the horrors that he experienced there.

> On my first day, the leather strap
> Went epileptic in the Big Study,
> Its echoes plashing over our bowed heads

The word 'epileptic' reinforces the horror that the new boy felt. The instrument of torture seemed to have a mind of its own, it was uncontrollable. And the word 'plashing' as well as having an **onomatopoeic** (see Literary Terms) effect gives the sense of an engulfing pain that hurts them all.

*2. A Constable Calls*

The young Seamus Heaney in the background observes the interrogation carried out by the policeman. The constable has visited his father to record information about the crops grown on the farm.

The boy inspects the bicycle that the policeman has left outside, leaning on the window-sill. His eyes flit over all the details such as the mudguards, the handlebars, the dynamo and the pedals. His camera-eye pans inside to the constable's cap lying on the floor. Despite the routine nature of the visit the boy feels fear while his father is reciting the details. His eye focuses on the revolver in the policeman's belt.

The boy feels guilt when the father fails to mention the turnpike in the potato field and he imagines the cell in the barracks where his father might be imprisoned.

He observes the policeman's departure and his eye is drawn to the 'baton-case' on the man's belt. Seamus Heaney calls the policeman's ledger the 'domesday book'. The boy watches as the visitor says goodbye to him before cycling away. He hears the ticking of the bicycle as it moves off down the road.

COMMENT

*The poet creates images of fear.*

The poet expresses the fear that the young boy feels when the policeman calls. Words and phrases such as 'cocked back' (rifle ready to fire), 'boot of the law' (trampling nature of the constabulary), 'revolver butt' (threat of being clubbed or shot), 'black hole in the barracks' (the police cells where many of his nationalist friends spent time), evoke the atmosphere of terror and interrogation. He also compares the official ledger to the 'Domesday Book', a book that might provide evidence for his father's imprisonment if he were not completely honest with the authorities.

Thus we are aware that the poet is confronting the reader with a situation that is loaded with the symbols of oppression even though the actual situation is routine, two men doing their jobs without any feeling of threat or fear on either side. The reader is aware that the poet is creating two terror-laden viewpoints. Firstly we observe the overactive imagination of the young boy (as in 'Death of a Naturalist' and in 'Blackberry-Picking') who overreacts to the visit from the law. And then, secondly, we interpret the poet's main intention which is to create an awareness of the overriding hostility that exists between the law and the ordinary citizen.

*Look at the barriers between the police and the ordinary citizen.*

**4. Summer 1969**

The poet expresses his guilt for not being in Northern Ireland in Summer 1969 when the most recent bout of unrest began. He chastises himself for suffering 'Only the bullying sun of Madrid'. He is still in his own country, however, if only in spirit. His reading is of the life of James Joyce and the images are very like those that he encounters in Ireland.

*Consider the poet's duty to write for his people.*

In his conversations he is encouraged to touch his people and he is reminded of the violence at home when somebody discusses the death of the playwright Lorca at the hands of the Guardia Civil and also when television reports tell of bullfights and deaths. When he visits the museum in Madrid the painting 'Shootings of the Third of May' by Goya is a grim reminder of the horrors in Ulster, as are Goya's other paintings in another room.

COMMENT

Seamus Heaney writes very pointedly about the manner in which his society punishes its own innocent citizens – 'While the Constabulary covered the mob / Firing into the Falls' – and he insists on his own cowardice for not being there.

Ireland and Spain are part of the same tapestry linked through the images of brutality that the poet sees in paintings and on television. Conversations with acquaintances remind him of his responsibilities: '"Go back," one said, "try to touch the people."'

*Study the way the poet links the different kinds of brutality.*

The theme of society's inhumanity to its own people is continued when he writes about the killing of the Spanish playwright, Lorca, and the horrific subjects of Goya's paintings:

> Goya's 'Shootings of the Third of May'
> Covered a wall – the thrown-up arms
> And spasm of the rebel, the helmeted
> And knapsacked military, the efficient
> Rake of the fusillade.

Later he writes of the all-embracing nature of this violence against individuals:

> ... Saturn
> Jewelled in the blood of its own children,
> Gigantic Chaos turning his brute hips
> Over the world.

*Note Seamus Heaney's feeling of guilt because of his neutrality.*

The final two lines are further evidence of the condemnation which Seamus Heaney feels he deserves because of his neutrality and non-involvement. The condemnation comes in his description of the way in which Goya involved himself completely in the Spanish struggle unlike the poet himself – 'He painted with his fists and elbows, flourished / The stained cape of his heart as history charged'.

## 5. Fosterage

This poem is dedicated to the short-story writer, Michael McLaverty, who was headmaster at St Joseph's College where Seamus Heaney taught when he left university.

The poem is shot through with advice from McLaverty, advice that he gave the poet in 1962. He states the importance of description that reveals its object. Katherine Mansfield's comment, that she would ensure the reader could hear the squeak of a '*laundry basket*', is quoted to underline the importance of the advice. The short-story writer also admonishes the poet to be economical with words and he gave Seamus Heaney a copy of the '*Journals*' of Hopkins which were underlined to show how Hopkins wrote in terse, understated prose and verse. Seamus Heaney remembers the writer's patience and his encouragement.

COMMENT
McLaverty encourages the emerging poet not just to revel in language but to use it to communicate, to make it an exact science. Seamus Heaney remembers the two authors quoted by McLaverty, the poet and Jesuit priest, Gerard Manley Hopkins and Katherine Mansfield, the short-story writer. The words and works of the writers emphasise the advice of the mentor, that he must not let words get in the way of his meaning or his description. But the advice is also, and perhaps more significantly, to '… Go your own way. / Do your own work'.

*Seamus Heaney accepts the agony the writer must endure.*

The poet realises the 'pain' that he must endure if he hopes to write well and also the reverence that he must have for the art of poetry. The final lines are a tribute to his friend, to his patience, to his encouragement and his teaching:

> … He discerned
> The lineaments of patience everywhere
> And fostered me and sent me out, with words
> Imposing on my tongue like obols.

**6. *Exposure***
This is the final poem in 'Singing School' and in the collection *North*. It is an account of the poet's movement from Belfast to Wicklow.

The scene is cold and wet and darkness is drawing in. He is expecting to see the comet which he imagines will appear in a splash of crimson. Sometimes he can see a falling star but what he would really like would be to find a meteorite. Instead he walks on ordinary damp leaves and the wasted shells of autumn and as he walks he imagines himself as a warlike hero using his gift of poetry like a 'slingstone' in a useless effort to do some good.

*Can a poet be a hero?*

He ponders his responsibilities to his community and wonders why he writes. Is it for his own satisfaction, the praise of friends or perhaps as a retort to his enemies?

He hears voices in the rain that tell him of betrayals and of the gnawing away of principles but the individual drops bring him encouragement and tell him of the power of his poetry that will be lost.

He knows that he does not betray and he knows that he is not a prisoner of the forces around him. Instead he has become a rebel, hidden in the woods of his own mind protected from those who would damage him, by the intricacies of his poetry. His long exposure to danger has made him aware of any harm that is moving in his direction.

He realises that he has been so lost in his thoughts that he has missed the vibrating colour of the comet.

## COMMENT

*Study the isolation that the poet feels.*

We sense the isolation that the poet feels at the beginning of the poem. His sadness is all the greater because of the time of year with its aura of decay and dampness. His spirits are lifted momentarily by the expectation of the 'once-in-a-lifetime' comet which is due in the skies at any moment.

The poet is well aware of the problems as well as the advantages of maintaining his distance from the horrors of Northern Ireland. He is confused. He battles with the conflicting thoughts and concepts that crowd his mind.

His image of himself as a warlike hero, using his poetry as a weapon, soon dissipates into a questioning of his motives for writing. That further leads to the notion that he may have let his people down, given half-measures or indeed fallen away from the high ideals that he once had. But clearly, through all this, comes the assurance that the poetry is a 'diamond absolute'. He may not be able to see the 'pulsing rose' of the complete and blinding answer to the problems in Northern Ireland but through his questioning and probing he has arrived at some truth about the situation.

*The poet's doubts about his motives are put to flight.*

# FIELD WORK

## CASUALTY

The subject of this poem is Louis O'Neill, who spent most evenings in a public house. One of these pubs was owned by Seamus Heaney's father-in-law.

The poet describes how the man would order his drinks without speaking. His mimes were recognised because he was such a frequent visitor. He would leave at closing time dressed in a peaked cap and waders. A family man, who was not afraid of work, he was on the dole. Seamus Heaney liked the whole personality of the man, his movement, his keen observation and his awareness of all that was happening around him.

The man could not understand Seamus Heaney's life as a writer and when he did mention poetry the poet moved the conversation to fishing, the horse and cart or the IRA because he was afraid of patronising the man.

But the fisherman was only too aware of Seamus Heaney's tactics.

During an IRA curfew he was blown up by a bomb. That curfew was imposed after the massacre of thirteen Catholics in Derry. The poet describes the tension in Derry at the time.

*How blameworthy are ordinary citizens for their own suffering?*

The funerals tied people together on that bitterly cold day. His friend, however, would not be bound by anybody's rules and the curfew was not for him. On the night he was killed he went to a pub miles away because he loved the warm, noisy atmosphere. The poet asks the question 'How culpable was he' and he can hear the fisherman asking him to give him an answer.

Seamus Heaney did not go to the funeral but he describes the quiet rhythm of his friend's final journey. He remembers the day he was taken out by him on his fishing boat, a day of freedom.

He is abruptly returned to reality and he wishes that the fisherman was there to question him again.

## COMMENT

*How does the poet create the image of a solitary man?*

The poems open with an image of a solitary drinker who spoke little. He is a man who cares little for the rules of society. He is on the dole despite the fact that he is '… natural for work'. He poaches eels in forbidden waters. His whole demeanour is of a man who is constantly on the watch, a man who is outside the law. The poet has great affection for him:

> I loved his whole manner,
> Sure-footed but too sly,
> His deadpan sidling tact,
> His fisherman's quick eye
> And turned observant back.

The poet is aware that he might be patronising if he allows their conversation to dwell on poetry and gently he steers away from any talk of art. He talks instead of ordinary things such as fishing, farming or the actions of the 'Provisionals'.

Seamus Heaney recounts his death. He also underlines the fact that the rest of his community obeyed the unofficial dictat from the IRA that people stay indoors. The fisherman did not accept constraints from anybody in society and, in the end, he died because of this. The poet reports the massacre and comments on the community's reactions:

> PARAS THIRTEEN, the walls said,
> BOGSIDE NIL. That Wednesday
> Everybody held
> His breath and trembled.

But the solitary fisherman refuses to be cowed.

*How does the poet create the image of sadness at the funeral?*

The poet creates an image of cold bitterness as he describes the flow of coffins from the door of the cathedral. The picture is surreal as we see what appears to be an unending stream of coffins floating 'Like blossoms on slow water' all of which brought the watchers together in a:

> ... tightening
> Till we were braced and bound
> Like brothers in a ring.

But not Louis O'Neill. The warnings of his own people had no significance for him and neither had the black flags or the threats on the phone.

Seamus Heaney imagines his face, a face that will always stay with him, as the bomb goes off, imagines his terrified stare in the midst of death: 'His cornered out faced stare / Blinding in the flash.'

The poet asks to what extent the man was responsible for his own death:

'Now you're supposed to be
An educated man,'
I hear him say, 'Puzzle me
The right answer to that one.'

The fisherman's funeral is described as a slow, sad procession. It soon merges into a memory of the day he took the poet out on his boat, a day when the poet 'tasted freedom'. He links this experience to his life, his responsibilities as a writer and where the rhythm is leading him into the unknown:

... and smile
As you find a rhythm
Working you, slow mile by mile,
Into your proper haunt
Somewhere, well out, beyond ...

There is a poignancy to the opening line and the last three lines of the final section where he regrets his absence from the funeral and also wishes that this simple man was there again to question him:

I missed his funeral,

...

Dawn-sniffing revernant,
Plodder through midnight rain,
Question me again.

In the end is the real message of the poem that, without trying, this simple man has the answer to the problems of Northern Ireland? He goes about his business quietly, without bothering anybody, without taking sides.

# TEST YOURSELF (*North* and *Field Work*)

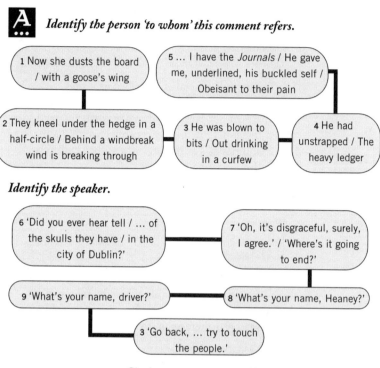

**A** *Identify the person 'to whom' this comment refers.*

1 Now she dusts the board / with a goose's wing

5 ... I have the *Journals* / He gave me, underlined, his buckled self / Obeisant to their pain

2 They kneel under the hedge in a half-circle / Behind a windbreak wind is breaking through

3 He was blown to bits / Out drinking in a curfew

4 He had unstrapped / The heavy ledger

*Identify the speaker.*

6 'Did you ever hear tell / ... of the skulls they have / in the city of Dublin?'

7 'Oh, it's disgraceful, surely, I agree.' / 'Where's it going to end?'

9 'What's your name, driver?'

8 'What's your name, Heaney?'

3 'Go back, ... try to touch the people.'

Check your answers on page 80.

**B** *Consider these issues.*

**a** Discuss the meaning of 'each neighbouring murder' in the poem 'Funeral Rites' and look at the concept in the light of other poems.

**b** From your reading of 'Viking Dublin: Trial Pieces', 'Bone Dreams' and 'Bog Queen' consider Seamus Heaney's thoughts about himself and his writing.

**c** What is the meaning of the title 'Whatever You Say Say Nothing'?

**d** Why is accent so important in Northern Ireland, according to the poet? (Read 'The Ministry of Fear')

**e** Why does the poet feel guilt in the poem 'Punishment'?

**f** How does Seamus Heaney show the conflict between the law and the ordinary Catholics in Northern Ireland? (Read 'A Constable Calls')

**g** Discuss the character of Louis O'Neill as he appears in 'Casualty'.

# Part three

# COMMENTARY

## THEMES

### LOSS OF CHILDHOOD INNOCENCE

The main theme in Seamus Heaney's first collection, *Death of a Naturalist*, is the loss of childhood innocence and his initiation into adulthood. The young boy is a naturalist in two senses. He is a naturalist because he is in tune with nature and he is also a naturalist because he is not yet tied down by the trappings of society. He behaves as he wishes, according to his intuition.

The young Seamus Heaney had the opportunity to explore nature and to enjoy that exploration. In 'Death of a Naturalist' he shows the pleasure he felt when experiencing the countryside in all its facets. He writes about the flax-dam, the blue-bottles, the dragon-flies and the butterflies:

> But best of all was the warm thick slobber
> Of frogspawn that grew like clotted water
> In the shade of the banks.

But soon he realises that this pleasure will not last when he sees the 'great slime kings' approaching to gain revenge for his theft of the tadpoles. The gentle world created by his teacher, Miss Mills, has been destroyed and with it much of the child's uninhibited pleasure.

In the poem 'Blackberry-Picking' the poet writes about the joy he and his friends experienced when harvesting the fruit. The voluptuous nature of their pleasure is soon dissipated, however, when the fruit begins to rot. Nature's promise is broken all too soon. The child's misery is all too evident in the last three lines:

> I always felt like crying. It wasn't fair
> That all the lovely canfuls smelt of rot.
> Each year I hoped they'd keep, knew they would not.

The death of his young brother and his father's despair as a result of the tragedy forces the teenager to assume adult responsibility.

The final poem in the collection, 'Personal Helicon', sees the poet accepting his mission to write poetry. This is what he will do as an adult. As a child he explored wells of all kinds in a free, haphazard way without any regard for rules, but now he realises that he has to have a reason to '… pry into roots, to finger slime'. The adult Seamus Heaney will '… rhyme / To see myself, to set the darkness echoing'.

In 'Follower' the poet writes about his relationship with his father. As a child he admired his father and wanted to follow in his footsteps – 'To close one eye, stiffen my arm'. But he soon lost this enthusiasm as he grew into adulthood. His father is now more of a nuisance rather than someone to be admired. When we read 'Digging' we discover that, yes, he does want to 'dig' as his father did but he will dig with his pen rather than with a spade.

There are other poems that deal with childhood and adulthood in later collections. In 'Anahorish' Seamus Heaney writes lovingly about his early school days and in 'A Policeman Calls' we see the young boy observing his father's interrogation and taking his parent's guilt on his shoulders.

The death of the naturalist in the poet creates conflicting emotions, regret for what once was and also a sense of freedom, the freedom to do what he really wants. It is this conflict that creates the poetry.

## HISTORY

The first of Seamus Heaney's historical poems is 'At a Potato Digging' which is not included in the *New Selected Poems*. The poem refers to the famine in Ireland which occurred during the years 1845-8 (see Context and Setting). The second historical poem is a 'Requiem for the Croppies' and refers to the climax of the great rebellion of 1798.

'At a Potato Digging' is a memorial to those who died as a result of the disaster but it also creates the image of modern-day potato pickers paying homage to the earth goddess in an effort to prevent such a tragedy ever happening again.

'Requiem for the Croppies' is a new beginning in the poet's opinion. He sees the seeds in the pockets of the dead rebels as the germ of further revolutions in the years to come, not unlike the aftermath of the Easter 1916 Rising and the huge wave of support that was created as a result of the execution of the leaders. Seamus Heaney commemorates the incidents that happened and the rebels who died in the service of their country. He also shows his peasant readers (for he was writing his version of history for the ordinary working people) that this struggle created equality. The social order was overthrown and we hear that 'The priest lay behind ditches with the tramp'.

The poet uses the technique of the ballad and the folk story to inspire his readers. The ballad-makers of the time told their stories using images from the countryside: rotting 'like a marrow', the blood on the hillside, the dying peasants who 'grubbing like plants in the bitch earth' (see 'At a Potato Digging'). The vision of a resurrected 'Croppie' coming back among his people to tell his horrific tale is a mixture of the ghost story and the folk tale so popular among the country people.

In the collection *North*, Seamus Heaney explores Ireland's past history in an attempt to understand the present. The exploration often creates nightmare images which merge, more often than not, into the grotesque visions of modern-day terrors. The last lines of 'Bog Queen' evoke flashes of the 'Croppies', the men of Easter 1916 and the Provisionals themselves. Like the 'Bog Queen' they have, **metaphorically** (see Literary Terms) speaking, lain in wait until the time was 'right' to rise up:

> The plait of my hair,
> a slimy birth-cord
> of bog, had been cut
>
> and I rose from the dark,
> hacked bone, skull-ware,
> frayed stitches, tufts,
> small gleams on the bank.

Again, in 'The Tollund Man', Seamus Heaney merges the past with the present. He tells the story of the four young brothers who were shot on the railway line and links their murders to the sacrificial nature of the death of 'The Tollund Man'.

Seamus Heaney turns time and again to the history of his people in an attempt to connect the present and the past. For him the seeds of the present troubles were sown in the past but he also suggests (in 'Funeral Rites' for instance) that, perhaps, if we look back into the very pagan origins of the Irish Nation we might find permanent solutions to the conflict in Ulster.

## WRITING AND LANGUAGE

Many of Seamus Heaney's poems study the art of writing. He realised very early on in his life that poetry could be a very powerful, energetic force but he was also aware that poetry would not necessarily change anything.

***The art of writing***

In the collection *Death of a Naturalist* the poet writes freely about the art of writing. In 'Digging' he informs the reader that he will use his pen to search for ideas and to explore his roots. 'Personal Helicon', the final poem in his first collection, makes us aware that this is a jumping-off point and he is now prepared to explore the unknown and dangerous. As a young boy he delighted in finding and looking into dark wells on the family farm. Now, as an adult, he explores the darkness through his poetry.

*Look at the importance of the sound and meaning of names.*

The names of places that were important to him as a child and an adult play a significant part in the poetry. We are not just talking about the places but also the sound and meaning of the names. The poet went to primary school in Anahorish and he describes the sound of the name in loving terms. He revels in the all-embracing feel of the word and it is fitting that he remembers the area as a secure and comfortable womb of a place. But it is not just the sound and feel of the word that holds so much for the writer, it is also the real meaning of the word. If we translate the original name (*anach fhior uisce*) we discover that it means 'the place of clear water' and it is apt that this should be the real name of the school where he found life, literature and his love of writing. Similarly, the name 'Broagh' translates into 'riverbank', a wet pliable place very suitable for a poet who wishes to dig below the surface.

*The poet is unsure about his goals and motives.*

The poet's lack of confidence in his writing and in what he is trying to achieve through his writing, surfaces in the collection *North*. He wishes that he could write in such a way that he would do something wonderful for his people, but in the poem 'Exposure', he finds himself questioning his motives for being a poet and, more specifically, his motives for being a poet of his people. Eventually he is reassured that his poetry is a medium that will stand the test of time.

When dealing with the troubles in Northern Ireland, Seamus Heaney could not encourage armed conflict for his Catholic friends and neighbours, but he could help to bind them together, could help to increase their sense of identity and this is, perhaps, his comfort, that his writing can go some way to achieving this.

# LANGUAGE & IMAGERY

Note the poet's use
of assonance,
alliteration and
onomatopoeia.

In the collection *Death of a Naturalist*, Seamus Heaney uses **alliteration, assonance** and **onomatopoeia** (see Literary Terms) to create the sounds of the farm and of his childhood. We hear the terrifying sound made by the frogs. The quiet whispering sounds overwhelm the child. The 's' sounds combined with the long vowel sounds create a malignant, unpleasant force: 'their loose necks pulsed like sails' ('Death of a Naturalist'). The consistent stress pattern produces the effect of the sinister breathing of the frogs or the 'slime kings' as Seamus Heaney calls them.

The poet uses alliteration and onomatopoeia to evoke the sounds of the spade digging into the 'gravelly' flowerbeds in 'Digging'. The alliterative effect of the 's' and 'g' sounds in the phrase 'clean rasping' create, very precisely, the noise of the spade as it entered the stony ground. This contrasts powerfully with the first two lines: 'Between my finger and my thumb / The squat pen rests; snug as a gun'. The opening is heavy with full vowel sounds and slow, almost cumbersome, consonantal sounds creating the impression that writing is much more laborious and indirect than the act of digging the soil.

*Images of
violence*

There are many images of violence in the poems. In 'Digging' we are immediately struck by the **simile** (see Literary Terms) of the gun and the pen. The ghost of the rebel in 'Requiem for the Croppies' evokes the terrible massacre on Vinegar Hill using phrases such as: 'Terraced thousands died', 'shaking scythes at cannon', 'hillside blushed' and 'soaked in our broken wave'.

Seamus Heaney finds himself involved in the pain of the victims in 'Tollund Man' and in 'Punishment'. The suffering of his people in Northern Ireland merges into the pain experienced by the 'Little adultress' and by 'The Tollund Man'.

Much of the vocabulary used by the poet is physical. In 'Blackberry-Picking' the look and feel of the fruit is created in the phrases 'glossy purple clot', 'red, green, hard as a knot' and in 'Digging' the 'cool hardness' of the potatoes becomes real. The tactile nature of the words and phrases is, perhaps, most obvious in the collection *Death of a Naturalist* but it is also a very important quality of the poetry in *North* as we see when we read 'A Constable Calls' and 'Summer 1969'.

# PART FOUR

# Study Skills

## How to use quotations

One of the secrets of success in writing essays is the way you use quotations. There are five basic principles:

- Put inverted commas at the beginning and end of the quotation
- Write the quotation exactly as it appears in the original
- Do not use a quotation that repeats what you have just written
- Use the quotation so that it fits into your sentence
- Keep the quotation as short as possible

Quotations should be used to develop the line of thought in your essays.

Your comment should not duplicate what is in your quotation. For example:

**Seamus Heaney compares his pen to the gun: 'The squat pen rests: snug as a gun'.**

Far more effective is to write:

**Seamus Heaney emphasises the power and danger of the pen when he says: 'The squat pen rests: snug as a gun'.**

Always lay out the lines as they appear in the text. For example:

**'Right down the dam gross-bellied frogs were cocked On sods; their loose necks pulsed like sails'.**

or:

**'Right down the dam the gross-bellied frogs were cocked / On sods; their loose necks pulsed like sails'.**

However, the most sophisticated way of using the writer's words is to embed them into your sentence:

**When the poet tells us that they found 'A rat-grey fungus, glutting on our cache' he is emphasising the revulsion felt by the children.**

When you use quotations in this way, you are demonstrating the ability to use text as evidence to support your ideas.

Everyone writes differently. Work through the suggestions given here and adapt the advice to suit your own style and interests. This will improve your essay-writing skills and allow your personal voice to emerge.

The following points indicate in ascending order the skills of essay writing:

- Picking out one or two facts about the story and adding the odd detail
- Writing about the text by retelling the story
- Retelling the story and adding a quotation here and there
- Organising an answer which explains what is happening in the text and giving quotations to support what you write

..................................................................

- Writing in such a way as to show that you have thought about the intentions of the writer of the text and that you understand the techniques used
- Writing at some length, giving your viewpoint on the text and commenting by picking out details to support your views
- Looking at the text as a work of art, demonstrating clear critical judgement and explaining to the reader of your essay how the enjoyment of the text is assisted by literary devices, linguistic effects and psychological insights; showing how the text relates to the time when it was written

The dotted line above represents the division between lower and higher level grades. Higher-level performance begins when you start to consider your response as a reader of the text. The highest level is reached when you offer an enthusiastic personal response and show how this piece of literature is a product of its time.

*Coursework* Set aside an hour or so at the start of your work to plan
*essay* what you have to do.

- List all the points you feel are needed to cover the task. Collect page references of information and quotations that will support what you have to say. A helpful tool is the highlighter pen: this saves painstaking copying and enables you to target precisely what you want to use.

- Focus on what you consider to be the main points of the essay. Try to sum up your argument in a single sentence, which could be the closing sentence of your essay. Depending on the essay title, it could be a statement of the poem: 'In "Blackberry-Picking" Seamus Heaney creates the nightmare images of a childhood that is disappearing and adolescent insecurity fast approaching'; a comment on the poet's technique: 'The poet's feelings are understated in "Mid-Term Break" until the final devastating line which leaves us in no doubt about the bitterness felt by Seamus Heaney'; or a summary of the underlying theme: 'The main theme of "Personal Helicon" is the poet's assertion that he is going to be a writer who takes risks and who is going to explore the deep places of the mind.'

- Make a short essay plan. Use the first paragraph to introduce the argument you wish to make. In the following paragraphs develop this argument with details, examples and other possible points of view. Sum up your argument in the last paragraph. Check you have answered the question.

- Write the essay, remembering all the time the central point you are making.

- On completion, go back over what you have written to eliminate careless errors and improve expression. Read it aloud to yourself, or, if you are feeling more confident, to a relative or friend.

If you can, try to type your essay, using a word processor. This will allow you to correct and improve your writing without spoiling its appearance.

*Examination essay*

The essay written in an examination often carries more marks than the coursework essay even though it is written under considerable time pressure.

In the revision period build up notes on various aspects of the text you are using. Fortunately, in acquiring this set of York Notes on *Seamus Heaney Selected Poems*, you have made a prudent beginning! York Notes are set out to give you vital information and help you to construct your personal overview of the text.

Make notes with appropriate quotations about the key issues of the set text. Go into the examination knowing your text and having a clear set of opinions about it.

In most English Literature examinations you can take in copies of your set books. This is an enormous advantage although it may lull you into a false sense of security. Beware! There is simply not enough time in an examination to read the book from scratch.

*In the examination*

- Read the question paper carefully and remind yourself what you have to do.
- Look at the questions on your set texts to select the one that most interests you and mentally work out the points you wish to stress.
- Remind yourself of the time available and how you are going to use it.
- Briefly map out a short plan in note form that will keep your writing on track and illustrate the key argument you want to make.
- Then set about writing it.
- When you have finished, check through to eliminate errors.

*To summarise, these are the keys to success:*

- Know the text
- Have a clear understanding of and opinions on the storyline, characters, setting, themes and writer's concerns
- Select the right material
- Plan and write a clear response, continually bearing the question in mind

# SAMPLE ESSAY PLAN

A typical essay question on *Seamus Heaney Selected Poems* is followed by a sample essay plan in note form. This does not present the only answer to the question, merely one answer. Do not be afraid to include your own ideas and leave out some of the ones in this sample! Remember that quotations are essential to prove and illustrate the points you make.

**Discuss Seamus Heaney's childhood and loss of innocence as portrayed in *Death of a Naturalist*.**

*Part 1*
*Introduction*

General comment on the secure happy childhood and the pain of oncoming adolescence.

*Part 2*

a) Relationship with father:
- Admiration for father (and grandfather)
- Wishing to follow in footsteps
- Now wants to write, not farm the land
- Father now stumbling behind him
- Has to take adult responsibility when father can't cope with tragedy

Look at the poems 'Digging', 'Follower', 'Death of a Naturalist' and 'Mid-Term Break'.

b) Innocence of the free spirited young boy and the loss of this innocence:
- Love of nature
- Security of home and school life
- Acts according to instincts

- Nightmare images which destroy security
- Nature's 'revenge' and broken promises

Look at the poems 'Death of a Naturalist', 'Blackberry-Picking', 'Follower' and 'Digging'.

c) The explorer and the writer:
- The wells of his childhood
- The fear of the unknown
- What the adult must do

Mainly discussed in 'Personal Helicon'.

**Part 3**
**Conclusion**

Consider how Seamus Heaney deals with the following themes:
- Into the future
- Loss of innocence but also sense of freedom

# FURTHER QUESTIONS

Make a plan as shown above and attempt these questions:

1 Discuss Seamus Heaney's relationship with members of his family as portrayed in 'Digging', 'Follower' and 'Mid-Term Break'.
2 Choose any three poems by Seamus Heaney and discuss the contradictions that are an essential part of his poetry.
3 Read again the poems 'Requiem for the Croppies' and 'Tollund Man'. Write about the violent images in both poems and discuss the way in which the poet links the events of the past with the present troubles in Northern Ireland.
4 Louis O'Neill is the subject of 'Casualty'. Write a comment on the poem and on what conclusions it draws about Northern Ireland.

5   Read 'Whatever You Say Say Nothing', 'The Ministry of Fear' and 'A Constable Calls' and discuss the reactions of Seamus Heaney and others to the soldiers and the constabulary.

6   Comment on Seamus Heaney's treatment of Viking corpses and the bodies found in the bogs of Ireland and how he relates their history to his own time. Read 'Viking Dublin: Trial Pieces', 'Bog Queen' and 'Punishment'.

7   Write a commentary on 'Funeral Rites' and on 'North'. Compare and contrast the poet's use of history.

8   What is the poet saying to us in 'Exposure'? Comment on Seamus Heaney's thoughts about his writing.

# PART FIVE

# CULTURAL CONNECTIONS

## BROADER PERSPECTIVES

You have now read a short history of Ireland, studied the poems of Seamus Heaney with the help of the summaries and become aware of some of the broader themes in the Commentaries.

Now it is worthwhile to look briefly at some of the collections of Seamus Heaney's poetry that we have not discussed. *Station Island* (1984) is set on an island which has been a place of pilgrimage for a thousand years. The character is on a pilgrimage himself and eventually comes through to face the problems of the present. *The Haw Lantern* (1987) explores the theme of loss and particularly the death of his mother. Other poems in the collection are meditations on the conscience of the author. Seamus Heaney's most recent collections are *Seeing Things* (1991) and '*The Spirit Level*' (1996). This latter collection was published after he had been awarded the Nobel Prize for Literature.

Seamus Heaney has also written a number of prose volumes which give insight into the character and writing of the poet. All collections have been published by Faber and Faber.

Many books have been written about Seamus Heaney's poetry. The most accessible commentary is *Seamus Heaney* by Ronald Tamplin (Open University Press, 1989). The author discusses all collections up to, and including, *Station Island*.

A number of programmes have been broadcast by the BBC Schools service and will no doubt be found in English Faculty libraries.

For the serious student it is important to have a thorough knowledge of Irish history, at least from the twelfth century onwards. *The Oxford History of Ireland* edited by R.L. Foster (Oxford University Press, 1989) is a comprehensive and stimulating account of Irish history and should help the student to a more thorough understanding of many of Seamus Heaney's poems.

Finally, the daily papers, which report the modern day events in Northern Ireland, are essential reading.

**alliteration** a series of repeated consonantal sounds in a stretch of language

**assonance** the repetition of the same vowel sounds in neighbouring words

**couplet** a pair of rhymed lines

**foot** section of a line of verse

**free verse** verse without any regular pattern of stresses and line lengths

**half-rhyme** imperfect rhyme (e.g. 'escaped' and 'scooped'). Also called a pararhyme

**iambic** referring to a foot of verse consisting of a weak stressed syllable followed by a strongly stressed one

**iambic pentameter** line of five iambic feet, the most common metre pattern in English verse. Unrhymed iambic pentameter, called blank verse, was used a great deal by Shakespeare

**imagery** language in which metaphors and similes are used to cover all words appealing to the senses or feelings

**imperfect rhyme** see half-rhyme

**metaphor** figure of speech in which something is spoken of as being that which it resembles

**metre** regulated succession of groups of syllables creating a pattern. It is based on the use of long and short or stressed and unstressed syllables

**onomatopoeia** use of words whose sound helps to suggest the meaning

**pararhyme** see half-rhyme

**plot** plan of a novel or play. It should go beyond telling what has happened, and should suggest the basic pattern of interrelationships between the characters and between the events in the story

**rhythm** variation in the level of stress placed on syllables

**simile** poetic image which compares two things by pointing out the similarities between them. It should always contain the word 'as' or 'like'

**stanza** a unit of several lines of verse; a repeated group of lines of verse

# TEST ANSWERS

**TEST YOURSELF (*Death of a Naturalist*)**

**A** 1 Miss Walls *('Death of a Naturalist')*
2 The angry frogs *('Death of a Naturalist')*
3 Seamus Heaney's father *('Follower')*
4 Seamus Heaney's dead brother *('Mid-Term Break')*
5 Seamus Heaney's grandfather *('Digging')*
6 Seamus Heaney's father *('Digging')*
7 Seamus Heaney's father *('Mid-Term Break')*

**TEST YOURSELF**

**(*Door into the Dark* and *Wintering Out*)**

**A** 1 The Tollund Man *('The Tollund Man')*
2 The dead rebel *('Requiem for the Croppies')*
3 The turf cutters *('Bogland')*

4 The farm helpers *('Anahorish')*
5 The bride *('Wedding Day')*
6 The guests *('Wedding Day')*

**TEST YOURSELF (*North* and *Field Work*)**

**A** 1 Mary Heaney *('Sunlight')*
2 The Seed-Cutters *(The Seed Cutters')*
3 Louis O'Neill *('Casualty')*
4 Seamus Heaney's father *('A Constable Calls')*
5 Michael McLaverty *('Fosterage')*
6 Jimmy Farrell *('Viking Dublin: Trial Pieces')*
7 Seamus Heaney and his friends *('Whatever You Say Say Nothing')*
8 A priest at Seamus Heaney's school *('The Ministry of Fear')*
9 A policeman *('The Ministry of Fear')*
10 Friends in Madrid *('Summer 1969')*